LOVE IS US

To TOM: I'm so LUCKY to LOVE you.

Published by Sellers Publishing, Inc.
Copyright © 2019 Sellers Publishing, Inc.
Illustrations © 2019 Becca Cahan
All rights reserved.

Sellers Publishing, Inc.
161 John Roberts Road, South Portland, Maine 04106
Visit our website: www.sellerspublishing.com ● E-mail: rsp@rsvp.com

Mary L. Baldwin, Managing Editor

Charlotte Cromwell, Production Editor

ISBN 13: 978-1-4162-4674-9

10 9 8 7 6 5 4 3 2 1

Printed in China.

LOVE IS US

illustrated by BECCA ▲ CAHAN

SELLERS
PUBLISHING

Love is a story
& we get to write a
NEW CHAPTER
every day.

Love is
SPLITTING
the LAST donut
in the box.

Love is
AGREEING
on which

SHOWS
to binge–watch
TOGETHER.

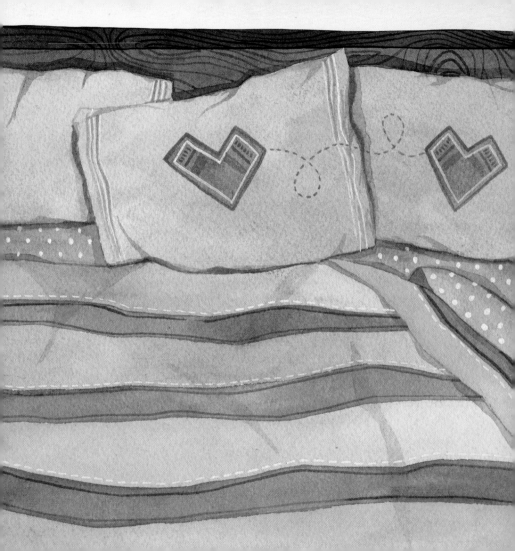

Love is bringing each other

COFFEE

on days we don't feel like getting out of bed.

Love is
TAKING TURNS
walking

the dog.

Love is making
each other

LAUGH.

Love is
DRESSING
UP

together

for Halloween.

LOVE IS

tolerating each other's

CRAZY

RELATIVES.

LOVE IS

shutting off

our phones &

PLAYING board games all weekend.

Love is
FINISHING

each other's
SENTENCES.

LOVE IS

pretending each other's

SILLY JOKES

are hilarious.

Love is not eating

ICE CREAM

if one of us

is trying to be

SUGAR-free.

Love is

Making
a HOME

together.

Love is building a fire
together & sitting beside it
all NIGHT long.

Love is **TENDING** our garden together.

Love is about enjoying the

ROAD TRIP

rather than counting
the hours to our

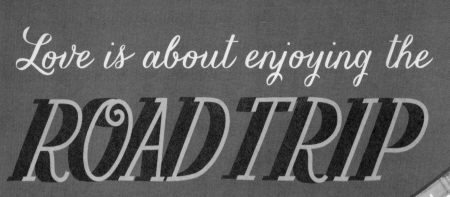

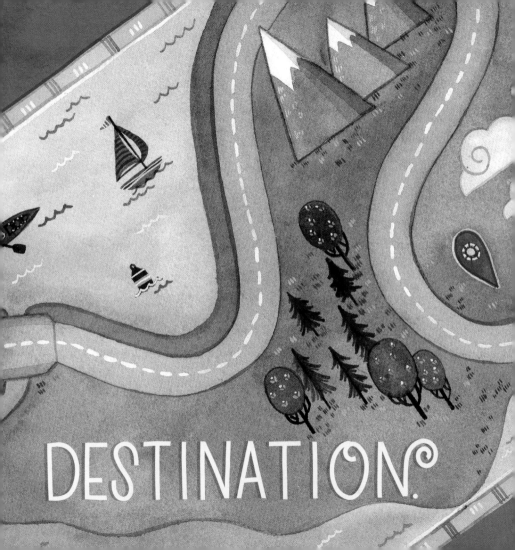

Love is going on
spontaneous
adventures
together

Love is ENCOURAGING each other to

go beyond our
COMFORT
ZONES.

Love is one
LEAP OF FAITH
after another...and catching
each other if we leap
too far.

LOVE IS

➤➤➤➤ *being* ➤

each other's

PROTECTOR.

Love is
SUPPORTING
one another's
DREAMS &
ASPIRATIONS.

Love is wanting to do things

TOGETHER

but knowing

that doing things

a part

IS OKAY.

LOVE IS
remembering that
feelings
are often more

important than
words or
THOUGHTS.

Love is
TRUSTING
each other

with our

SECRETS.

Love is **SUPPORTING** *each other in* **GOOD TIMES & BAD.**

Love is remembering
that forgiving brings us
➤ CLOSER, ➤

blaming pushes us

A P A R T.

Love is remembering that relationships are like *trees*. The more they can *BEND*, the less likely they are to *BREAK*.

Love is
understanding that to have a

WONDERFUL
PARTNER,

you have to be a
wonderful partner.

LOVE IS knowing that if we had to choose again, we'd still

choose
EACH
OTHER.